First World War
and Army of Occupation
War Diary
France, Belgium and Germany

19 DIVISION
58 Infantry Brigade
Duke of Edinburgh's (Wiltshire Regiment)
2nd Battalion
1 May 1918 - 28 February 1919

WO95/2093/1

The Naval & Military Press Ltd
www.nmarchive.com
Published in association with The National Archives

Published by

The Naval & Military Press Ltd

Unit 10 Ridgewood Industrial Park,

Uckfield, East Sussex,

TN22 5QE England

Tel: +44 (0) 1825 749494

www.naval-military-press.com

www.nmarchive.com

This diary has been reprinted in facsimile from the original. Any imperfections are inevitably reproduced and the quality may fall short of modern type and cartographic standards.

© Crown Copyright
Images reproduced by permission of The National Archives, London, England, 2015.

Contents

Document type	Place/Title	Date From	Date To
Heading	WO95/2093-1		
Heading	19th Division 58th Infy Bde 2nd Bn Wiltshire Regt May 1918-Feb 1919 From 30 Div 21 Bde		
Heading	War Diary Of The 2nd Battalion Wiltshire Regt From 1st May. 1918 To 31st May. 1918 Volume 44		
War Diary	Le Paradis Nr St Omer	01/05/1918	13/05/1918
War Diary	Herzeele	14/05/1918	16/05/1918
War Diary	Rexpoede	17/05/1918	18/05/1918
War Diary	Vesigneul-Sur-Marne	19/05/1918	28/05/1918
War Diary	Vesigneul	28/05/1918	28/05/1918
War Diary	Chambrecy	29/05/1918	29/05/1918
War Diary	In Action	30/05/1918	30/05/1918
War Diary	In Action Nr Chambrecy	30/05/1918	31/05/1918
Heading	War Diary of The 2nd Battn. Wiltshire Regt. For Month Of June. 1918. Vol 42		
War Diary	In Action Near Chambrecy.	01/06/1918	06/06/1918
War Diary	Bois de Courton.	06/06/1918	12/06/1918
War Diary	Chamuzy.	13/06/1918	18/06/1918
War Diary	Bois De Courton.	19/06/1918	19/06/1918
War Diary	Hautvillers.	20/06/1918	20/06/1918
War Diary	Cramant.	21/06/1918	21/06/1918
War Diary	Le Mesnil Broussy.	22/06/1918	30/06/1918
Heading	War Diary of 2nd Bn Wiltshire Regiment From 1st to 31st July 1918 Volume 46		
War Diary	Vassimont	01/07/1918	03/07/1918
War Diary	Coupelle Vielle	04/07/1918	04/07/1918
War Diary	Campagne	05/07/1918	11/07/1918
War Diary	Auchy Au Bois	12/07/1918	31/07/1918
Heading	War Diary of The 2nd Battalion Wiltshire Regiment. From 1st to 31st August 1918 Vol 44		
War Diary	Auchy-Au-Bois	01/08/1918	06/08/1918
War Diary	Hinges.	07/08/1918	10/08/1918
War Diary	Chocques	11/08/1918	14/08/1918
War Diary	Hinges	15/08/1918	31/08/1918
Heading	2nd Bn Wiltshire Regiment War Diary For September 1918 Volume 48		
War Diary	Field Near Locon	01/09/1918	02/09/1918
War Diary	Near Locon.	03/09/1918	05/09/1918
War Diary	Hinges	06/09/1918	10/09/1918
War Diary	Richbourg St Vaast	11/09/1918	22/09/1918
War Diary	Hinges	23/09/1918	29/09/1918
War Diary	Le Touret	30/09/1918	30/09/1918
Heading	War Diary of The 2nd Battn. The Wiltshire Regiment October 1918 Volume 25		
War Diary	Sains. Les. Pernes	01/10/1918	04/10/1918
War Diary	Gouy In Ertois	05/10/1918	07/10/1918
War Diary	Graincourt	08/10/1918	08/10/1918
War Diary	Cantaing.	09/10/1918	10/10/1918
War Diary	Cambrai	11/10/1918	13/10/1918
War Diary	Cagnoncles.	14/10/1918	16/10/1918

War Diary	Rieux	17/10/1918	18/10/1918
War Diary	Staubert.	18/10/1918	23/10/1918
War Diary	Rieux	24/10/1918	31/10/1918
Heading	War Diary of 2nd Bn Wiltshire Regiment From 1st to 30 November 1918. Volume 50		
War Diary	Rieux	01/11/1918	02/11/1918
War Diary	Vendegies.	03/11/1918	03/11/1918
War Diary	Nr Jenlain.	04/11/1918	05/11/1918
War Diary	Maison Blanche.	06/11/1918	06/11/1918
War Diary	Meaurain	07/11/1918	08/11/1918
War Diary	Breaugies	09/11/1918	10/11/1918
War Diary	Eth	11/11/1918	14/11/1918
War Diary	St Martin	15/11/1918	15/11/1918
War Diary	Avesnes	16/11/1918	25/11/1918
War Diary	Cambrai	26/11/1918	29/11/1918
War Diary	Fieffs	30/11/1918	30/11/1918
Heading	War Diary of 2nd Bn Wiltshire Regiment From 1st to 31st December 1918. Volume 51		
War Diary	Fieffs.	01/12/1918	12/12/1918
War Diary	St Leger.	13/12/1918	31/12/1918
Heading	War Diary of 2nd Bn. Wiltshire Regiment From 1st to 31st January 1919 Volume 52		
War Diary	St. Leger.	01/01/1919	31/01/1919
Heading	War Diary of 2. Bn. Wiltshire Regiment From 1st to 28 February 1919. Volume 52		
War Diary	St Leger.	01/02/1919	24/02/1919
War Diary	Villers L'Hopital	25/02/1919	28/02/1919

WO 97/2093 (1)

19TH DIVISION
58TH INFY BDE

2ND BN WILTSHIRE REGT
MAY 1918-FEB 1919

FROM 30 DIV 21 BDE

WAR DIARY

OF THE

2ND BATTALION WILTSHIRE REGT

FROM

1ST MAY, 1918

TO

31ST MAY, 1918

VOLUME 44.

2/1 B Wiltshire Regt

WAR DIARY
or
INTELLIGENCE SUMMARY.
(Erase heading not required.)

Army Form C. 2118.

Instructions regarding War Diaries and Intelligence Summaries are contained in F.S. Regs., Part II. and the Staff Manual respectively. Title pages will be prepared in manuscript.

Place	Date 1918 MAY	Hour	Summary of Events and Information	Remarks and references to Appendices
LE PARADIS nr ST OMER	1st		A party of 3 Officers (Lieut S COWIER, 2/Lt W.M. LANGLER and E.G. PENN) and 50 O. Ranks proceeded to WATOU (WEST OF POPERINGHE) by bus forming part of a Bde Composite working party for trench digging etc in the neighbourhood of WATOU.	
do	2nd		Quiet day. Nothing of importance to report	
do	3rd		"	
do	4th		"	
do	5th		all quiet. Nothing to report	
do	6th		2nd Lts 2/Lieut E.G. PEAR to hospital from Bde Composite working party and 2/Lt E.W. PAYNE to hospital from Composite Battn	
do	7th		all quiet. Nothing to report	
do	8th		Working party under Lt. S COWIER returned from WATOU	
do	9th		Quiet day. The party the total of which 6/5 galliers and A.C. DAVIE and 7L SHARLAND attacked to 2nd BEDFORDSHIRE Regt rejoined in the evening. That party consisted of 2/Lieut E.S. GALLIERS and A.C. DAVIE and 7L SHARLAND. It was ascertained that this party had been in action on the 8th inst. Sustained the following casualties: 2/Lieuts E.W. PLUMMER and E.K. HATTON wounded. 7 O Ranks killed, 6 wounded and 37 missing.	
do	10th		Quiet day. Battalion resting + cleaning up	
do	11th		La nuit fine. no yesterday	
do	12th		A Thursday Church Service was held at 10.30 in the Village Church, BUYSSCHEURE. Battalion resting. Owing to the serious ill. of Lieut S COWIER and the gassing of Capt MAJ H.O. JONES M.C. proceeded to 2nd/3rd Bn Wilts. Lieut S COWIER awaiting orders of a/adjutant.	
do	13th		This morning Battalion paraded 1.30 p.m and inspected by Lt. Col MERVILLE Gen. Staff, who pointed out and explained with the C.O. Br WILTSHIRE Regt (Bde Duties Staff) the officers and 509 Other Ranks were taken on en strength to the Bde Drawing Staff for the Division. 26 officers and 509 Other Ranks were taken on our strength	

2nd Bn [illegible]

WAR DIARY
or
INTELLIGENCE SUMMARY.
(Erase heading not required.)

Army Form C. 2118.

Instructions regarding War Diaries and Intelligence Summaries are contained in F. S. Regs., Part II. and the Staff Manual respectively. Title pages will be prepared in manuscript.

Place	Date 1914 MAY	Hour	Summary of Events and Information	Remarks and references to Appendices
HERZEELE	14th		Bn. [?] Orders issued from Brig. The Battalion paraded at 9.30 a.m. for inspection by the Commanding Officer Lieut. Col. G.F.E. RABIGH.	
do	15th		Company training under two own arrangements	
do	16th		Inspection and fatigues. Battalion paraded at 11.30 p.m. and marched to REXPOEDE, where it entrained at 4.30 a.m. and went from Sur-Mer travelling all by night.	
REXPOEDE	17th			
	18th		Journey continued. Arrived at CHALONS-SUR-MARNE (South of RHEIMS) at 6.15 p.m. and thence marched via MAIRY-SUR-MARNE and ST. GERMAIN to billets at VESIGNEUIL-SUR-MARNE. Letters by 9.30 p.m.	
VESIGNEUL-SUR-MARNE	19th		Disturbing during the same was held at 10 a.m. Battalion resting remainder of day.	
	20th			
	21st		Companies training under their own arrangements.	
	22nd		Lord's Service.	
	23rd		Same service.	
	24th		Church parade 9 a.m. Lieut. G.D. CHAPMAN admitted to hospital sick.	
			Captain carrying out parties Aug Bull. P.T and B.F. Tactical Schemes. Lieut H.S. KEMSHEAD assumed duties of Adjutant vice Lieut S. COLLIER who resumed duties of Signalling Officer.	
	25th		As no service was yesterday.	
	26th		Church Service was held at 9.30 a.m. in "A" Coy. parade ground. Battalion resting remainder of day. Lieut J. Arnton and received that Lieut. G.B. RIMINGTON had been granted the training Corps. Capt. (A/Lt. Col.) H.S. HODGES M.C. appointed from 21st Bn. and assumed duties of Adjutant. Lieut H.S. KEMSHEAD resuming duties of recount Adjutant.	
	27th		Companies training under two own arrangements. Orders were received about 11.30 p.m. that the Battalion was to be in readiness to move at one hours notice.	
	28th		Battalion marched off at 10.30 a.m. and proceeded to SUVIGNY. Battalion ready to assembly arrived at 7.30 p.m. the Battalion was informed by telephone that it would entrain	

Army Form C. 2118.

2nd Battalion

WAR DIARY
or
INTELLIGENCE SUMMARY.
(Erase heading not required.)

Instructions regarding War Diaries and Intelligence Summaries, are contained in F. S. Regs., Part II. and the Staff Manual respectively. Title pages will be prepared in manuscript.

Place	Date 1918 MAY	Hour	Summary of Events and Information	Remarks and references to Appendices
VESIGNEUL	27th cont.		as retiring heard arrived forward to reconnoitre situation, with a strength of 20 Officers & 500 ORs. As the Command would retreat at VESIGNEUL SUR-MARNE and neighbouring Battalion outlawed to Battalion at right, and that night the Batt. actioned at the Cave Road between BLIGNY and CHAMBRECY. The G.O.C. 19th Inf. Bde. ordered the Commanding Officer to take up a position on the heights N.W. of BLIGNY as an outpost for the defence of the Brigade. One outpost line was taken up. 1 at 12.30am. the Brigade ordered the Battalion to move to BLIGNY, before this order could be carried out further orders were received by the Battalion to proceed to & retire.	
CHAMBRECY	29th		near K.18 of SARCY and assist in the defence of the Battalion in the SORCY Kauer. About 2 p.m. the Company Officers were ordered to move to the Battalion on the POISY and take up a position in the high ground N. of BOUILLE as a rearguard from the Batln. which offered less resistance and reduced to a force of 1000 yd. "B" & "C" Companies in front line with "B" Company in Reserve. The Battalion immediately organised its new position. The position kept them from any surprise on the wing immediately in	
			the sector. Heavy fighting was then in progress on the wings, and in the neighbourhood of TRESLON and GERMIGNY. Later the shelling of B.8h. & 25h. Brigades compelled to retreat from the front and were ordered to retire on line B.17h.18h. on our line had been the front line and except for a little shelling by Field Guns all was very to be quiet. No enemy infantry were sighted by the Commanders (Major L. SHEPPERD N.C.) and 4 Officers and 163 other ranks which was left behind at VESIGNEUL SUR MARNE were 1h. Off. of B.30 am. and proceeded via ST GERMAIN - CHEPI and MONCETZ to SORRY joining the Battalion there.	
In action	30th		The enemy attacked in the early morning but found as forced up on our front by our flank who were heavily engaged. We forced to give ground. B. Coy. of the Battalion held by the Expt. (Major Irwin attd.) to move forward together and fight hand about winning own flank had been forced back and shortly afterwards a big machine gun could	

2nd Wiltshire Regt
WAR DIARY
INTELLIGENCE SUMMARY.
(Erase heading not required.)

Army Form C. 2118.

Place	Date 1918 MAY	Hour	Summary of Events and Information	Remarks and references to Appendices
In action	30th		action near the aerodrome at GERMIGNY harassing our line and entering on that line.	
CHAMBRECY		Co.M.	at 2.25 pm the Battalion which is astride the ridge running E of SARCY, thickened and effected in good order under some difficulty owing to hostile M.G. fire, and it is believed 1 officer and 16 O.Rs were cut off. The Battalion was commenced to organize a position between the road E & J SARCY site the effects of the Brigade = E.J SARCY. The CHESHIRES were on our Right and the SHROPSHIRES and STAFFS on our Right. The enemy quickly followed this up moving under cover & pushing forward him M.G. and lorries & their was our night flank to withdraw to a position on our right flank then became involved and we suffered many casualties eventually withdrawing to a position S.W. of BLIGNY with our left on the River ARDRE which was fortified by 2/punab. 2 Thumas and N. Grindley were killed. Lieut. L.G. Dudley 2/lieut. Dundas M. Bidwell and W.T. Baker wounded and 2 and R.G. Denham missing. At about 7.30 hrs the Major sorted of all the orders the Battn to return to its former position S of SARCY. The Battalion then returned with a view of acting as escorts up to the Brigade H.Q. at SARCY and found the French in position. After remaining for about 3 hours through its in turn the position was reconnoitred a position later arrived from the 56 Bde ordering the Battalion to retire to its position S.W. of BLIGNY. The Battalion retired to latter to its position about 3.30 am. The G.O.C. 56 Bde then informed the O.C. Battalion that the battalion was in reserve and would be for some attack as required should it be used. The Battalion remained in this position until 5 pm when the Brig. Major brought instructions for it to counter attack to turn on the road Bois N.J. CHAMBRECY and the high ground N.W. of CHAMBRECY village. The Company Officer-Cdt. assembled to plans and orders the Battalion for the attack. The attack not launched at 7.20 pm. Very considerable MG fire was met with	
do	31st		from and N. J. CHAMBRECY but finally with the help of Artillery fire all the Battalion personally led by	

2/6 Wiltshire

WAR DIARY or INTELLIGENCE SUMMARY

Army Form C. 2118.

Place	Date	Hour	Summary of Events and Information	Remarks and references to Appendices
So Posten An CHAMBRECY	1918 MAY 31st		The Coy. ???? Officer pressed on to the objectives which it reached in the course passing up with the Reserve on the Left flank. The position was rapidly consolidated in the heavy fire with remnants of the Battalion reinforced by enemy's own cavalry rejected by only 5 officers remaining and about 120 men. Capt R.S. GALLIERS had killed 2/Lieut A.E.M. WELSFORD, A.J. OSBORNE, T.A.C. DAWE and H.H. HILL wounded and 2/Lieut S.W.H. DANN missing. About 30-40 German had lay on the crest of the hill N.N of CHAMBRECY, and guarded a few at the farm in the valley. During the night the Israels sent up supports for our right flank which was then absent, and later a party of ROYAL WELSH FUSILIERS came up and linked up our right thus covering the position. The Battalion remained in this position all night and strengthened, consolidated and strengthened.	

H.B.J??? Captain Lt
for
Major
Comdg 2/6 Bn Wiltshire Regt

CONFIDENTIAL.

WAR DIARY

of the

2nd Battn. WILTSHIRE Regt.

FOR MONTH

OF

JUNE, 1918.

A.L. Thynne Lieut. Colonel,
Commanding 2nd Batt n/ Wiltshire Regiment.

5th July, 1918.

2nd Bn. Wiltshire Regt.

WAR DIARY
or
INTELLIGENCE SUMMARY

(Erase heading not required.)

Army Form C. 2118.

Instructions regarding War Diaries and Intelligence Summaries are contained in F. S. Regs., Part II. and the Staff Manual respectively. Title pages will be prepared in manuscript.

Place	Date 1918.	Hour	Summary of Events and Information	Remarks and references to Appendices
In action near CHAMBRECY.	June 1st		Liaison was established with the French on our Left, and it was agreed that each should inform the other of any orders regarding withdrawal if ordered. The enemy attacked the French heavily in the morning, and about 2 p.m. the French informed us that they were ordered to withdraw, thus exposing our Left flank. The Battalion, having received no orders, hung on, and about 4.30 p.m. enemy machine guns crept up on our Left and came into action, firing into the rear of our lines and enfilading Battalion Headquarters. About 7.30 p.m. the Battalion was ordered to withdraw and take up a position in front of the BOIS d'ECLISSE, joining up with the ROYAL WELSH FUSILIERS on the Right and the 8th GLOUCESTERS on the Left. This withdrawal was effected in small numbers and with covering fire under great difficulty, some 50 casualties being sustained. The Battalion then re-assembled and proceeded to take up the line as ordered, joining up with the ROYAL WELSH FUSILIERS on the Road CHAMBRECY - BLIGNY, and with the 8th GLOUCESTERS on the Left. The Battalion dug in on one line and carefully camouflaged the positions. The night was quiet except for shelling of back areas.	
do.	2nd		The Battalion remained in the same position all day, the enemy remaining more or less quiet. Much movement was observed in the neighbourhood of VILLE and IHERY. The Artillery were informed, and heavily engaged these targets, including some two or three known M.G. emplacements. The night was quiet, and was spent in organising the defence in depth, rear lines being dug and occupied as soon as completed.	
do.	3rd		Battalion remained in the same position. The front was quiet except for registration by enemy batteries. At 9 p.m. the 58th Composite Battalion was formed, composed of remnants of this Battalion, the 9th ROYAL WELSH FUSILIERS and 9th WELCH, under the command of Lieut. Colonel C. F. E. RAPSON. Strength of Battalion, about 14 Officers and 460 Other Ranks. The Battalion continued the digging of Support and Reserve lines, occupying same and thinning the Front line as soon as completed.	
do.	4th		The Battalion remained in the same positions and spent a quiet day. There was the usual artillery activity on the woods and roads, but the trenches escaped notice. At night work was continued on rear lines and all positions strengthened. At 10 p.m. the Battalion received warning that the enemy would probably attack in the morning on our Right flank, and possibly the attack would include our front as far South as CHAMPLAT. The warning was given to all ranks, and all precautions taken. Lieut. & Asst. Adjt. H. S. KEMSHEAD and 18 Other Ranks proceeded from the Surplus Personnel at SARRY to the line. The Surplus Personnel embussed at 9.30 p.m. and proceeded to LA MADELEINE (near VERTUS), arriving at 3.30 a.m.	

2nd Bn. Wiltshire Regt.

WAR DIARY

INTELLIGENCE SUMMARY.

(Erase heading not required.)

Army Form C. 2118.

Instructions regarding War Diaries and Intelligence Summaries are contained in F. S. Regs. Part II. and the Staff Manual respectively. Title pages will be prepared in manuscript.

Place	Date 1918.	Hour	Summary of Events and Information	Remarks and references to Appendices
In action near CHAMBRECY.	June 5th		Between 2 and 3 a.m. our artillery opened heavily on enemy gun positions and possible assembly lines. The enemy's artillery replied, shelling the woods and roads heavily. Casualties were slight. The Battalion "stood to" at 2 a.m. until well after daybreak, as there was a mist, but no attack developed. The day was quiet except for shelling by both artilleries. At night all positions of the Battalion were completed and thoroughly organised in depth, the Front line being held thinly. Enemy artillery was rather more active. Lieut. Colonel A. V. P. MARTIN, now Prisoner of War in Germany, awarded the D.S.O., vide the King's Birthday Honours.	
do.	6th		At about 2.15 a.m. the enemy artillery opened with great violence on the whole of the Front, and heavily bombarded our positions and the woods in rear. Our own artillery appeared to open at the same moment, putting down heavy counter barrage. The enemy used a large number of gas shells, which hung about the woods the whole day. The bombardment by the enemy's artillery, although very heavy, caused extremely few casualties, owing no doubt to the well concealed shell hole positions occupied by our men. The bombardment continued until about 4.15 a.m. when it appeared to be lifting. About 4.30 a.m. the enemy were seen to be advancing up the hill SOUTH of the CHAMBRECY Road in artillery formation, about 200 strong. Lieuts. S. COLLIER and H. W. MARSH seized the situation, got together about 30 to 40 men of the WILTS Company, and advanced to meet them under covering fire from our M.G's and rifles. These Officers then charged the enemy, who turned and ran, sustaining many casualties. A bugle was captured from one of the enemy by Lieut. COLLIER. The WILTS party then withdrew to its former position. By this time it had become light, and the situation was clearer. NORTH of the road the WELCH and ROYAL WELSH FUSILIERS Companies were rather more heavily engaged, and the enemy managed to obtain a footing in the small woods immediately NORTH of the CHAMBRECY Road, but here he was counter attacked and driven off. Severe casualties were inflicted upon him by all arms. Throughout the day he continued to attack the MONTAGNE de BLIGNY, obtaining lodgments occasionally from which he was continually forced out. The GLOUCESTERS reported at 10 a.m. that they had been attacked, but had driven off the enemy by M.G. fire, and said their positions were intact. The CHESHIRES on our Right flank withdrew a little, but on being reinforced regained their old positions, and reported all again in order at 10.30 a.m. The O.C. WILTS Company, in order to safeguard his flank, swung his Right flank round a little and reinforced the ROYAL WELSH FUSILIERS on the road. These positions were maintained all day, and handed over on relief at night (about 1.30 a.m.) to the 150th Bde. The Composite Battalion then withdrew to the BOIS de COURTON (Divsl. Reserve),	

2nd Bn. Wiltshire Regt.

Army Form C. 2118.

WAR DIARY
or
INTELLIGENCE SUMMARY.
(Erase heading not required.)

Instructions regarding War Diaries and Intelligence Summaries are contained in F. S. Regs., Part II. and the Staff Manual respectively. Title pages will be prepared in manuscript.

Place	Date 1918. June	Hour	Summary of Events and Information	Remarks and references to Appendices
BOIS de COURTON.	6th		arriving there between 4 and 5.30 a.m. Major W. S. SHEPHERD, M.C., joined the Transport Lines from the Surplus Personnel.	
do.	7th		Battalion resting and cleaning up in the BOIS de COURTON. The G.O.C. 58th Brigade and Staff Captain visited the Commanding Officer and congratulated him on the work of the Battalion. In the afternoon the Divisional General also called to see the C.O., who happened to be away at the time. The Divisional General highly complimented the Battalion on their excellent work. Major W. S. SHEPHERD, M.C. joined the 58th Composite Battalion and took over command, Lieut. Colonel G. F. E. RAPSON being ordered to the Transport Lines.	
do.	8th		Battalion remained in the BOIS de COURTON. The morning was spent in re-organising the companies, and a little close order drill. The 56th Brigade paraded in the wood for medal distribution by the Divisional General. Lieut. F. V. KELWAY was presented with the French CROIX de GUERRE, with palms. Lieut. & Asst. Adjt. H. S. KEMSHEAD joined the Composite Battalion and relieved Capt. & Adjt. H. B. JONES, M.C., who proceeded to the Transport Lines.	
do.	9th		Battalion remained in the BOIS de COURTON.	
do.	10th		Battalion in Divisional Reserve. The 1/6th CHESHIRES of the 25th Division, who were relieved on night 9/10th inst., joined the 58th Composite Battalion and formed a 4th Company. The Battalion was now composed of nr 4 Companies :- 2nd WILTSHIRES, 9th WELCH, 9th ROYAL WELSH FUSILIERS and 1/6th CHESHIRES, commanded by Major W. S. SHEPHERD, M.C., and H.Q. Staff of 2nd WILTSHIRES. The Battalion was under the 19th Division Composite Brigade, consisting of 56th, 57th and 58th Composite Battalions, and commanded by Brig. General HEATH, of 56th Brigade.	
do.	11th		A draft of 49 Other Ranks joined from Transport Lines.	
do.	12th		The 58th Composite Battalion relieved 151st Composite Battalion (50th Division) in Brigade Reserve in front of CHAMUZY in the evening. Lieut. Colonel G. F. E. RAPSON proceeded to the 6th Bn. WILTSHIRE Regt. Training Staff at LE TREPORT, and assumed command.	
CHAMUZY.	13th		Battalion in Brigade Reserve. Liaison with the 3rd ITALIAN Division on our Right was established. 2nd Lieut. A. SOUTHERN was wounded slightly. 7 men proceeded to the line from the Transport. Capt. A. J. SAMUT, M.C., 2nd Lieuts. J. N. GARDINER, B. C. HUNTER, G. M. JEANS, and J. ROBINSON joined Transport Lines from the Base.	

2nd Bn. WILTSHIRE Regt.

WAR DIARY
or
INTELLIGENCE SUMMARY.

(Erase heading not required)

Army Form C. 2118.

Instructions regarding War Diaries and Intelligence Summaries are contained in F. S. Regs., Part II. and the Staff Manual respectively. Title pages will be prepared in manuscript.

Place	Date 1918.	Hour	Summary of Events and Information	Remarks and references to Appendices
CHAMUZY.	June 14th		Battalion remained in Brigade Reserve. A working party of 1 Officer and 50 Other Ranks (CHESHIRE Company) were employed on carrying wire. 2nd Lieut. G. M. JEANS to Hospital Sick.	
do.	15th		Battalion in Brigade Reserve. 2nd Lieut. J. N. GARDINER joined WILTS Company from Transport Lines. A shell dropped in the Regimental Aid Post, Killing 3 Other Ranks and Wounding 8.	
do.	16th		Battalion in Brigade Reserve. The G.O.C. 19th Division, Major-General G. D. JEFFRIES, C.M.G. visited the Battalion.	
do.	17th		Battalion in Brigade Reserve. Major W. S. SHEPHERD, M.C., admitted to hospital with Trench Fever, Major BRADBURY, 9th WELCH, assuming command of 58th Composite Battalion. Italians of the 1/51st Battalion, 8th ITALIAN Division, reconnoitred our positions prior to the relief.	
do.	18th		The 58th Composite Battalion was relieved by the 1/51st Battn. ITALIAN Regt. of the 8th ITALIAN Division. The Composite Battalion moved back to the BOIS de COURTON, arriving at 3 a.m. At 5 a.m. the 58th Composite Battalion was broken up, and the remnants of the different Battalions were taken over by their own Headquarters. The 2nd WILTSHIRES, under Capt. A. J. SAMUT, M.C., moved back to the Transport Lines NORTH of HAUTVILLERS.	
BOIS DE COURTON.	19th			
HAUTVILLERS.	20th	7.30 a.m. 10 a.m.	Battalion paraded at 7.30 a.m. and marched via EPERNAY to billets at CRAMANT, arriving at 10 a.m. Battalion resting remainder of day.	
CRAMANT.	21st		Battalion, less Transport, paraded at 5.10 a.m. and marched to a point SOUTH of the village, where it embussed, and proceeded via VERTUS to LE MESNIL BROUSSY, arriving at 8.30 a.m. Transport left CRAMANT at 10 a.m. and moved by road, joining the Battalion at 7.30 p.m. Lieut. S. COLLIER proceeded to England on Leave.	
LE MESNIL BROUSSY.	22ND		Companies training under their own arrangements. Major W. S. SHEPHERD, M.C. and 2nd Lieut. G. M. JEANS rejoined from hospital. Major J. A. BUSFEILD, Lieut. J. H. F. RAMSDEN, 2nd Lieuts. L. F. HICKS, W. B. MAURAN, M. SILLARS, A. E. DAKIN, R. MILLER and Lieut. J. H. PEACOCK and 225 Other Ranks joined from Base.	
do.	23rd		Companies training under their own arrangements.	

2nd Bn. WILTSHIRE Regt.

WAR DIARY

INTELLIGENCE SUMMARY

(Erase heading not required.)

Army Form C. 2118.

Instructions regarding War Diaries and Intelligence
Summaries are contained in F. S. Regs., Part II.
and the Staff Manual respectively. Title pages
will be prepared in manuscript.

Place	Date 1918.	Hour	Summary of Events and Information	Remarks and references to Appendices
LE MESNIL BROUSSY.	June 24th		Companies training under their own arrangements, also bathing.	
do.	25th		Same routine. Lieut. Colonel Lord A. G. THYNNE, D.S.O., joined Battalion and assumed command, vice Major W. S. SHEPHERD, M.C.	
do.	26th		Companies training under their own arrangements.	
do.	27th		Same routine. 2nd Lieut. G. V. AUTON, D.C.M., joined for duty and posted to "D" Company.	
do.	28th		Same routine.	
do.	29th		Same routine.	
do.	30th		Battalion paraded at 9.20 a.m. and marched to VASSIMONT (distance 17 miles). A halt was made from 2 p.m. to 4 p.m. for dinners. Arrived and settled in billets by 6.15 p.m.	

5th July, 1918.

Lieut. Colonel,
Commanding 2nd Battalion Wiltshire Regiment.

Confidential

War Diary
of
2nd Bn. Wiltshire Regiment

From 1st to 31st July 1918.

Volume 46.

WAR DIARY
or
INTELLIGENCE SUMMARY.
(Erase heading not required.)

Army Form C. 2118.

Instructions regarding War Diaries and Intelligence Summaries are contained in F. S. Regs. Part II. and the Staff Manual respectively. Title pages will be prepared in manuscript.

Place	Date	Hour	Summary of Events and Information	Remarks and references to Appendices
VASSIMONT	1918 July 1st		Battalion resting and cleaning up.	
"	2nd		Battalion paraded at 1.15 am and marched to SOMMESOUS Station where it entrained at 3.30 am.	
"	3rd		Battalion detrained at ANVIN at 3 pm and marched via FRUGES to billets at COUPELLE VEILLE (distance 10 miles). Settled by 7 pm.	
COUPELLE VIELLE	4th		Battalion paraded at 10.15 am and marched to CAMPAGNE lez BOULONNAIS (about 11 miles). Settled in billets by 3 pm.	
CAMPAGNE	5th		Companies training under their own arrangements.	
"	6th		Companies training under their own arrangements. P.T. & B.F., Bombing and Lewis Gun Classes. 2nd Lieutenants J.H. DAWE, B.J.RIMMER, F.S.CORYN, G.BENNETT, H.J.PELHAM joined for duty. 2nd Lieut. G.D. CHAPMAN rejoined from Hospital.	
"	7th		Divine Service was held. Remainder of day resting.	
"	8th		Tactical Schemes carried out by Companies under supervision of Battalion Headquarters. Lewis Gun and Signalling Classes.	
"	9th		Company Training. Usual Classes. 2nd Lt L.F. HICKS rejoined from Hospital.	
"	10th		Same Routine. Orders received that Battalion would move to AUCHY AU BOIS tomorrow.	
"	11th		Battalion Transport moved off at 8.30 am. Battalion embussed at about 4 pm on SENLECQUES - MESNIL Road and proceeded to billets at AUCHY AU BOIS.	
AUCHY AU BOIS	12th		Training under Company arrangements. Capt P.P. LEGGE & 2nd Lt E.A. COLLING joined.	
"	13th		Same Routine. Officers and N.C.O's instructed under Staff Sergeant Major instructor of Musketry.	
"	14th		Sunday. Divine service was held at 9.30 am. Remainder of day resting. 2nd Lt S.C.JENKINS joined.	

Army Form C. 2118.

WAR DIARY
or
INTELLIGENCE SUMMARY.
(Erase heading not required.)

Instructions regarding War Diaries and Intelligence Summaries are contained in F. S. Regs., Part II. and the Staff Manual respectively. Title pages will be prepared in manuscript.

Place	Date 1918 July.	Hour	Summary of Events and Information	Remarks and references to Appendices
AUCHY AU BOIS.	15.		Training under Company arrangements. Section Leaders under Major W.S. Shepherd M.C.	
"	16.		Same routine except for "C" Company who carried out a Tactical Scheme under supervision of Battalion H.Q.	
"	17.		"D" and "C" Companies firing on Range. "A" and "B" Company carrying out Company Training. Lewis Gun, Signalling and Section Leaders Classes. Corporals and Lance Corporals Instructed under Regimental Sergeant Major in the afternoon.	
"	18.		Same routine.	
"	19.		Same routine except for "A" and "B" Companies firing on range.	
"	20.		Battalion Training. Battalion embussed at 8 am and proceeded to LOZINGHEM Training area for training. Returned to billets at about 5 pm. 2nd Lt COUCH joined for duty.	
"	21.		Sunday. Church Parade.	
"	22.		Training under Company arrangements - Usual Classes. Eliminating competition held by Battalion to select best Platoon for Brigade Competition. No. 4 Platoon "A" Company under 2nd Lt M AURAU selected. 2nd Lt YELLS and 2nd Lt DAVIES joined.	
"	23.		Battalion embussed at 8 am for LOZINGHEM Training Area. Returned to billets at about 4 pm. Lieut. H.C. WHITE and 2nd Lt R. PUGH joined.	
"	24.		Training under C company arrangements. Usual Classes.	
"	25.		"B" "C" "D" and Headquarter Companies on range. "A" Company carrying out a tactical Scheme.	
"	26.		"A" and "B" Companies on range - "C" and "D" Companies carrying out training under their own arrangements.	

WAR DIARY
or
INTELLIGENCE SUMMARY.
(Erase heading not required.)

Army Form C. 2118.

Place	1918	Hour	Summary of Events and Information	Remarks and references to Appendices
AUCHY AU BOIS	July 27.		Battalion route march - distance about 10 miles - leaving billets at 8 am and returning about 1 pm.	A.Ch.
"	28.		Battalion paraded at 7.45 with the object of proceeding to the LOZINGHEM TRAINING area but as lorries did not arrive Battalion returned to billets. Remainder of day resting.	A.Ch.
"	29.		Company Training - Usual classes.	A.Ch.
"	30.		"D" and "C" Companies on range - "A" & "B" Companies route marching. Usual classes.	A.Ch.
"	31.		Battalion inspected by G.O.C. Division after which the 21st Squadron R.A.F. gave a demonstration in order to practice all ranks in the use of the new Forward Area L.G. Sight. 2nd Lt BEHLO T joined and a draft of 28th Other Ranks.	A.Ch.

Alf Thynne
Lieut. Colonel.
Commanding 2nd Bn Wiltshire Regiment.

CONFIDENTIAL

WAR DIARY

OF THE

2nd Battalion WILTSHIRE REGIMENT.

From 1st to 31st AUGUST 1918

-o-o-o-o-o-o-o-o-o-o-o-o-o-o-o-o-o-

WAR DIARY
or
INTELLIGENCE SUMMARY.

(Erase heading not required.)

Army Form C. 2118.

Place	Date 1918. August	Hour	Summary of Events and Information	Remarks and references to Appendices
AUCHY-AU-BOIS.	1.		"A" and "B" Companies firing on the Range. "C" and "D" Companies route marching, Regimental Classes - Lewis Gun, Bombing, and Signalling.	MK
	2.		"C" & "D" Companies on range, "A" & "B" Companies Company Training, usual classes of instruction.	MK
	3.		"A" & "B" Coys on range, "C" Coy carried out Tactical Scheme, "D" Coy Company Training.	MK
	4.		Sunday. - Church Parade.	MK
	5.		Platoon Training in morning, remainder of day spent in organising the Battalion for the trenches.	MK
	6.		Battalion moved to trenches in relief of 1st GORDONS embussing at about 3 p.m. at AUCHY. Battalion debussed at CHOCQUES, had tea and waited until dusk before moving forward to the line.	MK
HINGES.	7.		Battalion in Outpost Line N.E. of HINGES. "A" & "B" Coys front line (shell hole posts) and "C" & "D" Coys in Support trenches. At about 6 a.m. a wire was received from 4th Div on our Left that the enemy was withdrawing on their front and that they were pushing forward. Immediately we pushed out reconnoitering patrols - 2nd Lieut BENNEIN from the Left flank to keep in touch with 4th Div, and 2nd Lieut MAURAU ffrom the Right. Both patrols came under machine gun fire before advancing very far, and were forced to return. Enemy machine guns and snipers were found to be very much on the alert. At about 9 p.m. "B" Coy moved forward about 200 yards and found touch with 4th Div. thus straightening out our line. On "B" Coy's front machine guns were persistantly active from VERTBOIS FARM. The Artillery were called for and made excellent practise much to the discomfort of the Hun, who emerged in an undignified manner and made tracks from the place at the double.	MK
	8.		"A" Coy's patrol pushed out in the early morning and entered Farm about 400 yards to their front but were enfiladed by Hun enemy machine guns and forced to withdraw. 2nd Lieut W.B. MAURAU was wounded. About 3 a.m. a patrol from "B" Coy got as far as VERTBOIS FARM and finding it unoccupied established a post there. This was found to be untenable during the morning owing to heavy hostile shelling. No further advances were made during the day and on the night of the 8/9th "C" Coy relieved "B" Coy on the Left and "D" Coy relieved "A" Coy on the Right. 2nd Lieut I.G. DAVIES "A" Coy was killed by a shell.	MK

Army Form C. 2118.

WAR DIARY
or
INTELLIGENCE SUMMARY.
(Erase heading not required.)

Instructions regarding War Diaries and Intelligence Summaries are contained in F. S. Regs., Part II. and the Staff Manual respectively. Title pages will be prepared in manuscript.

Place	Date	Hour	Summary of Events and Information	Remarks and references to Appendices
HINGES	1918 August 9.		Captain H.A. GALE M.C. wounded badly in the head about 6 am. Line advanced during the day chiefly on the right. On the left hostile machine gun posts delayed our patrols and prevented them pushing without undue casualties. Several casualties were caused by gas shelling and also by machine guns and snipers.	JWK
	10.		In the early morning a forward patrol under 2nd LT SILLARS located enemy machine gun post in his field S. of VERT BOIS FARM. Leaving a portion of his patrol to keep in touch with enemy 2nd LT SILLARS returned to Company H.Q. to organise the attack. Under the covering fire of a Lewis Gun on his right flank and 4 rifle bombers firing No. 36. R.B. from the cup discharger on his left flank 2nd Lt SILLARS accompanied by 2nd Lt STROTHERS led the rifle section to the attack and rushed the post. The enemy fought stubbornly and refused to surrender - 12 of them were killed and 2 taken prisoner, none escaping. While it lasted the fight was fierce. Several of the enemy were knocked on the head with rifle butts. He displayed considerable skill both in the tactical disposition of his small force and in the intelligent use of the various platoon weapons at his disposal. Both 2nd Lt SILLARS and 2nd Lt STROTHERS led the men with great courage and dash and much needed and valuable identification was secured showing that the 2nd Guards Reserve Regiment were along our front. Both Officers were unfortunately wounded. During the day we also had the following casualties 2nd Lieut's T.C. DELLIOTT, S.C. JENKINS, F.J. YELLS all wounded, 2nd Lieut F.D. GORYN went down badly gassed. Battalion was relieved on night 10/11th by 9th Welch after having advanced our line in all about 100 yards.	JWK
CHOCQUES	11.		Battalion arrived in Brigade Reserve at CHOCQUES. Day spent resting and reorganising.	JWK JWK
	12.		"A" and "B" Coys on range. "C" and "D" Coy training under Company arrangements.	
	13.		Company training. Classes - scouts, signallers, Lewis Gun, 2nd Lt S. WVH. DANN rejoined from Hos.	JWK
	14.		Company parades and organising for trenches. Night of 14/15th battalion relieved 9th R.W.F. in Support Trenches N.E. of HINGES. Relief complete by 12.30 am 15th.	JWK
HINGES.	15.		Battalion in support trenches. Dispositions - "A" Coy 2 Platoons in SUFFOLK Line and 2 Platoons in CANAL Line. "B" Coy in GORDON LINE. "C" Coy in SUFFOLK LINE. "D" Coy CANAL LINE. G.O.C. Division visited Battalion H.Q. in the morning. O.P. established in GORDON Line. Enemy Shelled [illegible] HINGES during night 15/16th - casualties 2 other Ranks killed and 3 gassed. 2nd Lt R.W. CORE joined for duty.	JWK

WAR DIARY
or
INTELLIGENCE SUMMARY.
(Erase heading not required.)

Army Form C. 2118.

Place	Date	Hour	Summary of Events and Information	Remarks and references to Appendices
HINGES.	1918. August. 16.		Battalion in Support Trenches. G.O.C. visited Support Line in the morning. 2nd Lieut G.M. JEANS rejoined "A" Coy from XIII Corps Infantry Course. Work done in trenches during morning and carrying party provided at night.	
	17.		The Quartermaster visited the troops in the support trenches and when returning to Battalion Headquarters through HINGES was wounded in the finger. G.O.C. visited our lines in the morning and found them satisfactory except that one hungry sentry was caught eating a rabbit.	
	18.		Battalion in Support Trenches. on the night 18/19th 2nd WILTS relieved 9th R.W.F. in the front line. Relief complete 1.30 a.m. 19th. 2nd Lieut G.M. JEANS wounded.	
	19.		Battalion in Front Line. "A"Coy Right front Company, "B" Coy Left front Company, "C" Coy Left support, "D" Coy Right support. Patrols from "A" & "B" Coys went out at dawn to reconnoitre enemy positions but were held up by heavy machine gun fire. In the afternoon the G.O.C. rang up to say that the Bosche was retiring on our left and instructed us to push out patrols again. 2nd Lieut G.D.CHAPMAN "B" Coy took out a patrol and encountered the same opposition. 2nd Lieut CHAPMAN was wounded in the arm by a machine gun bullet and was evacuated to a Field Ambulance. On the right 2nd Lieut S.W.H.DANN of "A" Coy pushed forward about 300 yards and established a post. The Battalion on our right, the 8th GLOSTERS, pushed forward and established posts in line with us. On the left the 1st WARWICKS were being relieved by the 2nd SEAFORTHS, 4th Div., and did not move with us. Capt H.W.MARSH M.C. "D" Coy went down badly gassed. Lieut J.H.PEACOCK took over command of "D" Coy. During the	
	20.		early morning a man of "A" Coy surprised and captured a ration party of the enemy, which had lost its way and was approaching our line. 13 prisoners passed through the 57th Brigade and a Sergt Major was brought to Battalion Headquarters. Word was received that patrols were pushing forward from Battalions on our flanks. "B" Coy accordingly pushed forward to bring our left in line with the SEAFORTHS. A forward Battalion Headquarters in the ABERDEEN LINE and was manned by the Commanding Officer, Second in Command, Intelligence Officer, Signallers, and Runners and Scouts. G.O.C. visited advanced Headquarters in the morning. Meanwhile patrols had pushed forward along the whole line and had advanced so far that, owing to the Brigade boundary converging to a point, the 58th Brigade was squeezed out. At 2 p.m. orders were received from Brigade to withdraw the Battalion to the ABERDEEN and EDINBURGH LINES. Operation Orders were accordingly issued and the Companies withdrew by Sections at 10 minutes intervals. Battalion Headquarters moved back to GORDON HOUSE with the exception of the	

Army Form C. 2118.

WAR DIARY
or
INTELLIGENCE SUMMARY.
(Erase heading not required.)

Instructions regarding War Diaries and Intelligence Summaries are contained in F. S. Regs., Part II. and the Staff Manual respectively. Title pages will be prepared in manuscript.

Place	Date 1918 August	Hour	Summary of Events and Information	Remarks and references to Appendices
HINGES	20. (cont)		Intelligence Officer who remained in the advanced Headquarters in charge of Report Centre. At 10 p.m. an inter Company relief took place. "C" Coy relieving "B" Coy in the EDINBURGH LINE, "D" Coy relieving "A" Coy in the VERTBOIS LINE.	JEK
	21.		Battalion now in Reserve. Report Centre closed at 10 a.m. 57th Brigade only holding one Platoon frontage in the line, remainder of Division squeezed out. The troops were in great spirit. Remainder of day spent in resting.	JEK
	22.		Orders received for relief of 74th Division on our left. 57th Brigade now squeezed out. Battalion spent day reorganising, cleaning up etc. 2nd Lieut R.W.GORE to Hospital.	JEK
	23.		The 58th Brigade relieved 4th Division. Relief of Support Battalions carried out in daylight. commencing at 2 p.m. 2nd WILTS relieved 2nd DUKE of WELLINGTONS in the CANAL and EDINBURGH LINES. 9th R.W.Fus. relieved 1st WARWICKS on our left. On the night 23/24th 9th WELCH relieved 2nd SEAFORTHS in the front line.	JEK
	24.		Division has two Brigades in the line and one in Reserve. 2nd WILTS disposed as follows - "A" Coy CANAL LINE S.E. of PONT D'HINGES - "B" Coy CANAL LINE N.W. of PONT D'HINGES - "C" Coy in GORDON LINE for counter attack on the CANAL - "D" Coy holding a line of strong posts in the EDINBURGH LINE. Lieut Col. Lord A.G. THYNNE D.S.O. left for 8days French leave. Major W.S. SHEPHERD M.C. assumes command of the Battalion. Companies at work in trenches and collecting salvage. The Quartermaster proceeds on leave to England.	JEK
	25.		Battalion in Support trenches. Capt CANTAIN R.A.M.C. (M.O. i/c Battalion) returned from Rest House TROUVILLE. Companies at baths in CHOCQUES, one platoon at a time.	JEK
	26.		Battalion in Support trenches. Epidimic of diarrahoia (?) in Battalion. CANAL and GORDON LINES shelled at intervals with gas shells and H.E. "A" & "B" Coys find working parties for R.E'S (making strong points in the EDINBURGH LINE). Daily work on trenches continued.	JEK

Army Form C. 2118.

WAR DIARY
or
INTELLIGENCE SUMMARY.
(Erase heading not required.)

Instructions regarding War Diaries and Intelligence Summaries are contained in F. S. Regs. Part II. and the Staff Manual respectively. Title pages will be prepared in manuscript.

Place	Date	Hour	Summary of Events and Information	Remarks and references to Appendices
HINGES.	1918 August 27.		R.E. working party found by "B" & "C" Coys. All Companies collecting huge quantities of salvage. On night of 27/28th "C" Coy moved into CANAL LINE on left of "B" Coy for period during which trench was unoccupied through the relief of 9th WELCH by 9th R.W.F.	
	28.		Battalion still in support trenches. Daily routine of trench repairing, salvage work, and R.E. working parties. G.O.C. Division visited Battalion Headquarters and expected GORDON LINE.	
	29.		Routine as previous day. G.O.C. visited Battalion Headquarters in afternoon with news of imminent enemy retirement on our front.	
	30.		Usual routine and working parties. News of enemy retirement and advance of R.W.Fus. No hostile shelling during past 24 hours.	
	31.		2nd Lieuts. R.LEITH; W.F.VIRGIN and BALCH, joined Battalion for duty. 2nd Lieut.G.V.AUTON D.C.M. to depot for rest. On night of 31st Aug/1st Sept Battalion relieved 9th R.W.Fus. in Outpost Line.	

A.J. Thynne
Lieutenant Colonel
Commanding 2nd Battalion WILTSHIRE Regiment.

2nd Bn Wiltshire Regiment

Confidential

War Diary

for

September 1918.

Volume 48.

WAR DIARY
INTELLIGENCE SUMMARY

(Erase heading not required.)

Army Form C. 2118.

Instructions regarding War Diaries and Intelligence Summaries are contained in F.S. Regs. Part II. and the Staff Manual respectively. Title pages will be prepared in manuscript.

Place	Date	Hour	Summary of Events and Information	Remarks and references to Appendices
Field Near LOCON	September 1918 1		Battalion relieved 3rd Bn Royal Welsh Fusiliers in front line on night August 31/Sept 1st. Relief reported complete 1.30 am. Company dispositions "C" Coy Right front, "D" Coy Left front "A" Coy Left support, "B" Coy Right support. At 6.30am "C" Coy pushed forward & advanced their line about 300yards bringing them in line with "D" Coy on the left. The whole line then pushed forward patrols, these however had not advanced more than 200 yards before they were held up by heavy M.G. fire from many enemy positions. It was the strongest resistance the Battalion had encountered since coming in on this front. The G.O.C. visited Battn H.Qrs.& "D" Coy in the morning & in the afternoon he again visited Battn.H.Qrs. along with the Divisional Commander. About 10 am. Battn.H.Qrs. vacated their hole and moved across the LAWE River and established itself in old Bosche dugouts in a small orchard. There was considerable "wind up" in the Division as regards "Booby" traps, this was shared in no small measure by Battn.H.Qrs., the dugouts were very thoroughly searched by the "Booby Trap" R.E. specialists. Anti-Shelling precautions, owing to the fact that the dugouts were roofed with one thickness ofly of German paper sandbags, were taken in the form of a thin deep slit trench being dug in the rear of the orchard. 1 Artillery Liaison Officer and a 2 Welsh Officer for liaison with battalion on Left flank were accomodated at Battn.H.Qrs.	MK
	2		Patrols again pushed forward and opposition again encountered but not so serious as yesterday. "C" Coy pushed forward on the right in the attempt to clear a group of houses which had harboured enemy machine guns. With the assistance of T.M's and rifle grenades they made about 7 bosche run from one house and a Lewis Gun opening on them caused at least 5 to fall as casualties. During the day the whole line was advanced about 400 yards but resistance still being strong it was decided by the Divisional Commander to make a local attack on the following day. In the afternoon considerable "wind up" at Battalion H.Q. caused the visit of a battery Commander who wished to place his guns along the hedges of the orchard ready for the stunt. This lead to heated argument between all members of Headquarters and the gunner Officer and he was eventually led away to see a better position which would not jeopardise the safety of H.Q. The Welch Liaison Officer was relieved by 2nd Lt G.V. ANTON D.C.M. during the afternoon. Preparations for the attack occupied the whole evening and "C" Coy was relieved on the right of our front by 3 Companies of the Welch Regt and "A" and "B" Companies of our Battalion moved up and formed a 3 Company front on the right and left of "D" Company. "C" Company withdrew to a line just forward of Battalion H.Q.	MK

Army Form C. 2118.

WAR DIARY
or
INTELLIGENCE SUMMARY.

(Erase heading not required.)

Instructions regarding War Diaries and Intelligence
Summaries are contained in F. S. Regs., Part II.
and the Staff Manual respectively. Title pages
will be prepared in manuscript.

Place	Date 1918	Hour	Summary of Events and Information	Remarks and references to Appendices
Near LOCON.	Septr 3:		At 4 am Major Shepherd and the Intelligence Officer with a few runners and signallers moved forward to an advanced H.Q. in WELLINGTON POST to direct operations. Companies were reported in position on jumping off line at 4.30 am. At 5.30 am the artillery opened out and an intense barrage was put down about 200 yards ahead of our front line. This was nobly backed up by the Machine Gun Corps. The barrage lasted 3 minutes and then advanced at rate of 100 yards every two minutes to 1st objective where it played continuously for 5 minutes. Following the barrage came our men who overcame with ease the slight resistance offered in the first few hundred yards and gained the first objective in a quarter of an hour. The barrage them moved forward to the final objective and positions were established by our men. 5 machine guns were captured and about 50 prisoners. The Bosche replied feebly to our barrage. In the evening Bn H.Q. moved forward to a concrete dugout near HARROW POST but finding signs of tampering and the prospect of being blown up, the dugout was evacuated hastily at dusk and all H.Q. turned to digging in, in the open. Col THYNNE who had returned from leave the previous day returned to Battn H.Q. at about 10 pm.	
"	4th		During the day the Transport and Q.M. Stores moved forward to HINGES. 2nd Lt S.W.H. DANN wounded during the operations - 6 O.Rks killed and 17 O.R. Wounded. Early in the morning a new Bosche Dugout was found, apparently an evacuated Brigade H.Q. and Bn H.Q. moved up and occupied it at about 10 am. Booby trap R. E's were sent for and spent the greater part of day cutting out wires etc. Major SHEPHERD returned to Depot at 2 pm. During the morning the Companies re-adjusted their lines and pushed out posts in old Bosche front line. Battalion was relieved by 8th Gloucester Regt. Relief completed by 12.30 am on 5th.	
"	5th		Battalion marched back to HINGES arriving complete by 4.30 am. Companies occupied the CANAL LINE from PONT D'HINGES to AVELLETTE BRIDGE. A, B and C from left to right and "D" Coy in GORDON Line. The day was spent in cleaning up and resting.	
HINGES	6th		Baths allotted to Battalion and occupied the morning. Reaping parties commenced to cut crops between GORDON and CANAL Lines. 2nd Lt D.W. Davies rejoined the Battalion.	
"	7th.		Companies re-organised and commenced training. Capt P.P. LEGGE M.C. took over duties of A/Adjutant from Lt Kemshead. Lt Ramsden assumed command of "C" Coy.	

WAR DIARY
or
INTELLIGENCE SUMMARY.
(Erase heading not required.)

Army Form C. 2118.

Instructions regarding War Diaries and Intelligence Summaries are contained in F. S. Regs. Part II. and the Staff Manual respectively. Title pages will be prepared in manuscript.

Place	Date 1918	Hour	Summary of Events and Information	Remarks and references to Appendices
HINGES	Sept 8th.		Church Parade on Canal Bank.	
"	" 9th.		Battalion embussed at 7 am and proceeded to BOMY training area for training exercise under supervision of Corps. The day was spoilt by continued rain and the Battalion returned drenched at about 4.30 pm.	
"	" 10th.		Battalion prepared for the line - embussed at HINGES CHURCH at 3.30 pm and were taken to ZELOBES POST from which we marched in to relieve the 3rd Worcester Regt. in support to the left Brigade Section. Battalion H.Q. occupied a trench crossing St MARYS ROAD slightly West of RICHBOURG St VAAST. Relief was by daylight and complete by 7.30 pm. The night was quiet.	
RICHBOURG St VAAST	" 11th		The morning opened with an enemy shoot on St MARYS ROAD and unfortunately Battn H.Q. came in for a few "Shorts". A/Corpl CORTEZ awaiting commission was killed and 2 other H.Q. Runners was wounded. Companies were spread across the Brigade line of retention in posts and commenced to build strong points under direction of R.E's. Hun artillery active at counter battery work caused considerable trouble to the Companies.	
"	" 12th		Work continued on strong points. A dugout in St VAAST Dump, luckily unoccupied was blown up by "booby trap".	
"	" 13th		Work continued under R.E's but hampered by rain. Day generally quiet.	
"	" 14th		Heavy guns shelling on line of retention caused gas casualties to 2nd Lt DAKIN and 7 O.Rks R.E. work continued at intervals throughout the day. Enemy and own artillery very active all day and 10 O.Rks were wounded. At 7.30 pm the Companies commenced relief of 9th Welch in front line. Col. THYNNE, Lt COLLIER and Capt CAMPAIN R.A.M.C. with 5 O.Rks when proceeding to front line Battan H.Q. were caught in a Counter battery straffe and the Colonel and Lt Collier were killed - also 3 other Ranks - and the Medical Officer and 2 Other Ranks wounded. Lt Col KING, Cheshire Regt assumed Command of the Battalion, after relief was complete at 11.30 pm.	
"	" 15th		Battalion in Front line. 2 Coys "C" and "D" holding the outpost line each with two platoons	

WAR DIARY
or
INTELLIGENCE SUMMARY.
(Erase heading not required.)

Army Form C. 2118.

Instructions regarding War Diaries and Intelligence Summaries are contained in F.S. Regs, Part II and the Staff Manual respectively. Title pages will be prepared in manuscript.

Place	Date	Hour	Summary of Events and Information	Remarks and references to Appendices
	1918 Sept 15th		in the front or observation line and two platoons in close support. Remaining two platoons were distributed along the B LINE or MAIN LINE of RESISTANCE – B on the right and C on the left. The day passed quietly. At night C Coy pushed out patrols from the left front Platoon which was established in a mine crater and our "Old No Man's Land" and reconnoitred the old Bosche Front line. This was found to be unoccupied as long as the moon was up. Colonel THYNNE was buried at BETHUNE, the Corps Division and Brigade Commanders attending.	
	" 16th		Quiet day. During the day work was done on the B Line by A and B Coys. After dark "C" Coy again pushed forward patrols and this time occupied and established two Platoons in the old German Front Line (MILLS TRENCH). Capt Kelway "A" Company went down to Field Ambulance sick. Lieut Campkin and 2nd Lt Casey joined Battalion from Depot and were posted to "B" and "C" Coys respectively.	
	" 17th		Quiet day. Daily programme of work on B Line carried out by "A" and "B" Companies. At night patrols were sent out from both front Companies to reconnoitre enemy positions and wire. Hostile patrols were found to be active and the enemy holding his line in strength. Observation post established in lip of crater in "C" Coy front. Capt Pakeman joined from Depot and was sent to B Company.	
	" 18th		Usual work of revetting and duckboarding under R.E's in B Line carried out. At night inter Company relief took place. On the left "A" Coy passed through "C" Coy and established posts about 200 yards in front of old line.	
	" 19th.		G.O.C. Division visited Battalion Headquarters in morning and discussed a proposed Battalion attack on MAUDLIN TRENCH with Col KING. Later this was enlarged into a Brigade attack and fixed for the 21st. Col King decided to make a small stunt that night in order to bring up the right flank to a suitable jumping off line. Accordingly at 10 pm two Platoons of B Coy under 2nd Lts DAVIE and VIRGIN went over under a light shrapnel barrage. On the right 2nd Lt VIRGIN progressed favourably but on the left 2nd Lt DAVIE was badly held up by a thick belt of wire which was mostly covered with vegetation. Hostile machine guns prevented him cutting the wire and he was forced to withdraw. 2nd Lt DAVIE was shot through the neck and died almost immediately. Under orders from the Commanding Officer the right flank was withdrawn and original jumping off positions re-established.	

WAR DIARY
or
INTELLIGENCE SUMMARY.
(Erase heading not required.)

Army Form C. 2118.

Instructions regarding War Diaries and Intelligence Summaries are contained in F. S. Regs., Part II. and the Staff Manual respectively. Title pages will be prepared in manuscript.

Place	Date	Hour	Summary of Events and Information	Remarks and references to Appendices
	1918 Sept. 20th		This attack led to a Brigade Conference which was held at our Headquarters on this date. Lt Col Jones (commanding Brigade temporarily), Lt Col. Mc Graid, Artillery, Brigade Major, Staff Captain besides Col King and Major Bradbury of the R.W.F. attended and the proposed attack on the 21st was discussed. It was finally decided to postpone it (with sanction from Division) until the heavy artillery and trench mortars had cut the enemy's wire and smashed in his concrete machine gun emplacements. Accordingly at night the Commanding Officer took the right front Company and the Intelligence Officer the left and platoons were withdrawn about 300 yards in order to permit our heavies to fire on the enemy's wire. The Battalion front was held by 4 Platoons occupying Platoon posts at 300 to 400 yards interval between Platoons.	
	" 21st		Our heavies engaged MAUDLIN TRENCH in the afternoon. Usual work in trenches during day. At night Platoons in front line wired all their positions.	
	" 22nd		Quiet day. Battalion relieved at night by 1/4th K.S.L.I. Battalion relieved by 12 midnight, and marched back through LACOUTURE to rail head when they entrained and taken to AVELETTE. From there the Battalion Marched to HINGES.	
HINGES	" 23rd		Battalion in HINGES. Companies in billets and tents. Cleaning up during day. The Divisional Follies performed in the school in the afternoon.	
"	" 24th		Training under Company arrangements. Companies at Baths.	
"	" 25th		Companies training. Lewis Gunners on Range.	
"	" 26th		Foden at HINGES. All Battalion disinfected. Company Training.	
"	" 27th		Church Parade in morning. Usual Company training.	
"	" 28th		Battalion relieved 3rd Worcesters in the Line of Retention on the Right Brigade Front. Battalion entrained at AVELETTE at 5.15 pm. Train ran off the rails on the way and Battalion did not detrain at LE TOURET till 7.20 pm	

Army Form C. 2118.

WAR DIARY
or
INTELLIGENCE SUMMARY.
(Erase heading not required.)

Place	Date	Hour	Summary of Events and Information	Remarks and references to Appendices
LE TOURET	1918. Sept. 28th		Relief complete at 9.30 pm.	
"	" 29th		Battalion in Line of Retention - right to left "A" "C" "D" and "B" Companies. Companies at work wiring under R.E's.	
"	" 30th		Companies at work constructing posts and wiring under R.E. supervision. Advance parties of the 74th Division arrived.	

R L Beaw
Major
Commanding 2nd Bn Wiltshire Regiment.

No. 77
46

Confidential Diary
War of the
2nd Battn. The Wiltshire Regiment

October 1918

Volumn 25

Army Form C. 2118.

WAR DIARY
or
INTELLIGENCE SUMMARY.
(Erase heading not required.)

Instructions regarding War Diaries and Intelligence Summaries are contained in F. S. Regs., Part II. and the Staff Manual respectively. Title pages will be prepared in manuscript.

Place	Date 1918	Hour	Summary of Events and Information	Remarks and references to Appendices
SAINS LES PERNES	October 1st		Battalion relieved by 16 Suffolks and proceeded by Light Railway and march route to billets at SAINS LES PERNES arriving there about 11am on 2nd	
	2		Resting and generally cleaning up. Lieut Col. E.A. King DSO. MC. proceeded to 9 G.Gordons Regt to take command of that Regiment	
	3		Major P.S.L Beaver MC. joined Battalion and took over command. 2. Lt. E.H. Jones rejoined.	
	4		Battalion entrained at PERNES Station at 2.10pm for the CAMBRAI Front and detrained at SAVY LE BRET at about 10pm and proceeded by march route to billets at GOUY en ERTOIS.	
GOUY en ERTOIS	5		Usual company parades	
	6		Company training. Classes for Lewis Gun, Vickers, Bearers 2/Lt. R.W. Fowke rejoining from hospital.	
	7		Battalion entrained at BARLY at 3pm and proceeded to camp near GRAINCOURT arriving 12/6am 8th	
GRAINCOURT	8		Resting and generally cleaning up. At 9.45pm Battalion paraded and marched to bivouacs in sunken road near CANTAING. Draft of 58 Other Ranks joined.	
CANTAING	9		Usual company inspection, cleaning up trenches and generally improving them.	
	10		Battalion paraded at 1/58pm and marched to billets in CAMBRAI.	

WAR DIARY
INTELLIGENCE SUMMARY
(Erase heading not required.)

Army Form C. 2118.

Instructions regarding War Diaries and Intelligence Summaries are contained in F. S. Regs., Part II. and the Staff Manual respectively. Title pages will be prepared in manuscript.

Place	Date	Hour	Summary of Events and Information	Remarks and references to Appendices
CAMBRAI	11.		Battalion under orders to move at short notice. Glass time spent in training	
	12.		Bringing company of 4 Royal Physical Training Lectures to NCOs on Open Warfare, Rifle Sections etc. How to fit the new N°36 Rod Exchanger and how to make out of garment	
CAGNONCLES.	13.		Battalion arrived at 14.30 hour (3.0 pm) and picqueted by route march to CAGNONCLES.	
	14.		Bath. A little to Companies. Company Platoon training and several classes for specialists	
	15.		Company practising the formation of attack.	
	16.		Battalion moved to RIEUX at 1500 hour taking part in a Brigade tactical scheme on the way. 1st day Arrived at RIEUX about 1800 hours	
RIEUX	17.		Usual close inspection of companies. Cleaning up of kits and vicinity.	
	18.		Companies trained in Gas Drill. Cleaning up of billets continued. Battalion bearers	
ST AUBERT			Training under M.O. Battalion proceeded to the line in relief of 10th WARWICKS. "B" & "C" remained in billets in ST AUBERT with Bn HQ. the remaining two Companies "A" & "D" going forward not relieving the two right half Companies held 10th WARWICKS on the line. During the night officers and NCOs reconnoitred the ground in rear of our entrenched attack field HQ.	
	19.		In the morning slit trenches were dug in the high ground just West of the Raile Selle in rear of Battn HQrs. Day about in preparing for the attack. About 1500 hours a patrol went out from "D" Coy to see if the Railway Embankment was still held by the enemy. They managed to close that R. Selle but were fired on later, only the N.C.O. returning. 2/L Welford took out a second patrol later to bring in the wounded and managed to gain the Railway Embankment which was then found unoccupied by the enemy	

WAR DIARY
or
INTELLIGENCE SUMMARY.

Army Form C. 2118.

Place	Date 1916	Hour	Summary of Events and Information	Remarks and references to Appendices
	October 19 (cont)		The result was the Battalion assembled on the Railway Embankment and the Barrage Table was altered. At 1930 hours Battalion HQrs moved forward to its Battle Position. At 2200 hours A and C Companies moved forward to their assembly positions arriving there at 2339 hours.	
	20.		At 0200 hours the Barrage opened 200 yards in front of the Railway Embankment, where it remained for 44 minutes to synchronise with the Afo. in the Barrage of Bde. on the right. Several of these shells failed short with the result that the Battalion suffered several casualties from our own Barrage, 2/Lieut J.H.F.RAMSDEN being wounded, 2/Lieut P.J.SIMMONS being killed and Capt S.A. PAKEMAN M.C. being wounded. The night was dull and black. A and C Companies reached the Final objective at 0730 hours and D Company in support. B Company in Reserve. Little opposition was met with. Our casualties 3 Officers and 119 Other Ranks. About 1700 hours orders were received to advance the Front Line about 1000 yards. This was done of the attack and completed as by 02:00 hours without any opposition.	
	21.		At 0630 hours the left platoon of C Company was attacked by an enemy patrol of about 20. The Platoon was on the alert and the Hun was quickly driven off leaving	

WAR DIARY
or
INTELLIGENCE SUMMARY.
(Erase heading not required.)

Army Form C. 2118.

Place	Date 1916	Hour	Summary of Events and Information	Remarks and references to Appendices
	21. (cont)		1 Officer and 2 men killed and 1 man wounded and one taken prisoner. The platoon also captured a German automatic rifle. At 1600 hours orders were received that we were to be relieved by the 9th Bn. that night. The relief of the front line was completed by 2130 hours. The Battalion moving back and taking up position in line in support. Coys were disposed along Railway and trench "A" Coy and B.H.Q. being dug in along the Railway embankment. Batts. in Support "C" Coy. detailed to assist our tanks all and behind Running Eye. "D" Coy, in support.	
	22.		Day cleaning up and reorganising.	
	23.		At 0320 hours the 87th Brigade on our right in conjunction with the Canadian on their right attacked and subsequently gained all their objectives. A dummy barrage was put down on our front. The little counter shooting resulted that front was very quiet. Enemies seemed dazed and not realising that an attack was being carried out. Two/three prisoners without arms came in during the afternoon. Orders were received that the 19th that night we were going right through. The 6th Berks were relieving the 19th. The relief was carried out without a hitch and was complete without relief. Arriving at 2200 hours Coy withdrew without relief and marched independently back to RIEUX where they met guides who showed them to their billets. The whole Battalion had withdrawn by 22:40 hours and were in billets by 0100 hours 24th.	
RIEUX	24th 25.		Generally cleaning up and resting. Companies allotted tasks. Usual reorganising and a little training carried out. 2/Lieut. W.R. HUMPHREYS to Hospital.	
	26.		Company and Platoon training and usual Specialist classes. Church Parade for Battalion at 1000 hours.	
	27.		2/Lieut. E.J. WEBB and A/F. FRENCH Lieut. & Q.M. F. O'HANSON joined Battalion. to Hospital.	
	28.		Company and Platoon training in morning and usual classes. In the afternoon Battalion paraded for a demonstration to illustrate different stages of a flying aeroplant Aeroplane commenced at 1415 hours.	

Army Form C. 2118.

WAR DIARY
or
INTELLIGENCE SUMMARY.
(Erase heading not required.)

Instructions regarding War Diaries and Intelligence Summaries are contained in F. S. Regs., Part II. and the Staff Manual respectively. Title pages will be prepared in manuscript.

Place	Date 1918	Hour	Summary of Events and Information	Remarks and references to Appendices
	October			
RIEUX	29		Each Company practised a tactical exercise. 2/Lieut R. MILLER and the Padre (Revd. W.J.C. BARRETT) went to F.A. sick.	
	30		Battalion practised a tactical exercise	
	31		Company and Platoon training. Closed classes for Specialists.	

C.B. Shepherd Maj.
/O Lieut Colonel
Commanding 2nd/4th Wiltshire Regiment

Confidential

War Diary

of

2nd Bn Wiltshire Regiment

From 1st to 30th November 1918.

Volume 50.

WAR DIARY
or
INTELLIGENCE SUMMARY.
(Erase heading not required.)

Army Form C. 2118.

Instructions regarding War Diaries and Intelligence Summaries are contained in F. S. Regs., Part II. and the Staff Manual respectively. Title pages will be prepared in manuscript.

Place	Date	Hour	Summary of Events and Information	Remarks and references to Appendices
RIBUX	1918 Novr 1st.		Battalion took part in a Brigade Tactical Scheme under Divisional arrangements.	
	2nd.		Battalion paraded at 0600 hours at RIEUX to proceed to HAUSSY in conjunction with the Brigade. The 3 Battalions marched across country in parallel columns arriving at HAUSSY at 1000 hours. The Battalion remained here in barns until 1620 hours when it paraded and marched to VENDEGIES arriving there at 2130 hours and billeted for the night.	
VENDEGIES.	3rd		The Commanding Officer, Company Commanders and Intelligence Officer proceeded to MARECHES to reconnoitre assembly positions for an attack that was to take place on the 4th. At 1620 hours the Battalion Transport and surplus personnel marched from VENDEGIES to assembly positions which had been altered owing to a BOSCHE retirement during the night of the 2/3rd. Assembly positions were eventually reached at 0115 hours on the 4th. Battalion Headquarters were established at LA PATT OIE.	
Nr JENLAIN.	4th		Assembly positions reached at 0115 hours on the road running North of JENLAIN. The Battalion attacked under a heavy barrage at 0600 hours. Little opposition was encountered until the PETIT AUNELLE River was reached. This was overcome and all objectives reached by 1015 hours with slight casualties. 2nd Lt FRENCH Took out a patrol and captured 9 Prisoners. At 1200 hours strong patrols were pushed out with a view to clearing the village of ETH. Heavy Artillery and Machine Gun fire was met and patrols had to return. It was finally decided to put a barrage down and advance at 1650 - "C" & "A" Companies leading the attack. ETH was captured and a position taken up on the high ground to the East of it. "B" Company under 2nd Lieut. G.V. AUTON D.C.M. was detailed to mop up the village. This was done very successfully, 50 prisoners being captured from the Chateau. Total number of prisoners for the day were 60. Machine Guns captured 6. 2nd Lt W.F. VIRGIN "B" Coy was killed in the advance to the first objective.	
	5 th		The advance was continued at 0626 hours under a short barrage and line pushed forward to ROISIN. Patrols were afterwards pushed out to road 1000 yards East of MAISON BLANCHE. When this objective was reached the Royal Welsh Fusiliers who had been in support jumped through us and the Battalion then became left support Battalion, Battalion H.Q. being established at MAISON BLANCHE.	

NOVEMBER 1918 - SHEET No.

Army Form C. 2118.

WAR DIARY
or
INTELLIGENCE SUMMARY.
(Erase heading not required.)

Instructions regarding War Diaries and Intelligence Summaries are contained in F.S. Regs. Part II. and the Staff Manual respectively. Title pages will be prepared in manuscript.

Place	1918 Nov.	Hour	Summary of Events and Information	Remarks and references to Appendices
MAISON BLANCHE.	6th.		The Battalion moved at 0430 hours to support the R.W.F's who were attacking at 0550 hours. Battn Companies were in position before Zero occupying the high ground West of BETRECHIES. Battn H.Q. moved forward to MEAURAIN.	A
MEAURAIN	7th	0930	At 0930 hours the 9th Bn Welch Regt relieved us thus making the Battalion support Battalion. Afterwards the Battalion moved back to MEAURAIN to billets.	A
"	8th	0930	At 0930 hours orders were received to moved forward to HOUDAIN just North of BAVAY but these orders were cancelled and the Battalion proceeded to BREAUGIES. The Brigade now came in reserve.	A
BREAUGIES	9th		The day was spent in resting and cleaning up and partial re-organisation.	A
"	10th		Orders were received to move to ETH. Billets in ETH were reached at 1145 hours. Remainder of day spent in rest and improvements to billets. General G.D. JEFFREYS C.B., C.M.G. Commdg the Division issued a Special Order conveying thanks to all ranks. Total Casualties during the attack - 1 Officer Killed - 2 Officers wounded. Other ranks - killed 31, wounded 142, missing 1.	A
ETH	11th	0930	At 0930 hours a verbal message was received from Brigade saying that hostilities would cease at 1100 hours. This was confirmed by wire ants at 1000 hours. The Battalion paraded and played outside billets for one hour to commemorate the cessation of hostilities. The civil population of ETH was overjoyed and shared in the general rejoicing. The village church bell which had been hidden from the Germans for four years was unearthed and rung for some time, the sound of it mingling with the Battalion Band. The Officers then on the strength of the Battalion were, Lieut. Col. P.S.L. BEAVER M.C. Major W.S. Shepherd M.C., Capt A.J. Sammut M.C. Capt P.P. Legg M.C., Capt J.H. Peacock, Lieut. E. Hoggarth, 2nd Lt H.T. Hockey MM. 2nd Lieut E.J. Webb, 2nd Lt J. Robinson, 2nd Lt G.V. Auton D.C.M., 2nd Lt A.F. French, 2nd Lt W.A. Humphreys, 2nd Lt B.C. Hunter, 2nd Lt L.W.L. Langer, 2nd Lt D.W. Davies. Lieut. C.B. de Forest (R.R.C., U.S.A) Medical Officer, 2nd Lt E.D. Galpin (Signalling Officer attached from 9th Bn Royal Welsh Fusiliers) and Revd W.B.C. Barrett. Those not with the Battalion were, Capt F.V. Kelway, 2nd Lt I. Fraser M.C. and 2nd Lt A.E.M. Welsford on leave, Lieut H.S. Kemshead on course, 2nd Lt E.H. Bosich on course, Lt & Q.M. E. O'Hanlon, 2nd Lt R.W. Gore	A, Barrel A

WAR DIARY
or
INTELLIGENCE SUMMARY.
(Erase heading not required.)

Army Form C. 2118.

Instructions regarding War Diaries and Intelligence Summaries are contained in F. S. Regs., Part II. and the Staff Manual respectively. Title pages will be prepared in manuscript.

Place	Date 1918	Hour	Summary of Events and Information	Remarks and references to Appendices
ETH	Novr 12th		and 2nd Lt R. Leith in hospital.	
	13th		The whole of the day spent in cleaning up. Transport was inspected by Major W.S. Shepherd M.C.	
	14th		The day spent in cleaning up, kit inspections and salving material.	
St MARTIN	15th		The Battalion moved by route march to St MARTIN near BEARLERAIN parading at 1015 hours and arriving at St MARTIN at 1645. Capt Kelway rejoined from leave.	
AVESNES	16th		Battalion moved by route march to AVESNES les AUBERT parading at 0925, arriving at AVESNES at 15.30.	
			Baths. The following Officers joined Battalion for duty.- 2nd Lieutenants M.E. MILLER, W.R. EDWARDS, J. DREWETT, C.A. POCOCK, R.C.H. CONNOLLY, W. YEO and R.G. MORTIMER.	
"	17th		Sunday - CHURCH PARADE.	
"	18th		Arm drill and Physical training under Company arrangements. Class of Corporals and Lance Korporals under the Regimental Sergeant Major. Companies inspected by the Commanding Officer during the morning.	
"	19th		Usual routine - Training under Company arrangements. 2nd Lt J. COUCH rejoined from Hospital. 2nd Lt C.F. Casey rejoined.	
"	20th		Training under Company arrangements.	
"	21st		Battalion paraded at 1000 hours for rehearsal of Parade by G.O.C. Brigade taking place the following day. 2nd Lt A.S. EDWARDS and 2nd Lt W.R. WEST joined for duty. 2nd Lt R.W. Gore rejoined for duty.	
"	22nd		Battalion paraded at 0910 hours for inspection by G.O.C. 58th Brigade.	
" "	23rd) 24th)		Training under Company arrangements. Afternoons devoted to cleaning of equipment etc.	

NOVEMBER 1918 - SHEET No.

Army Form C. 2118.

WAR DIARY
or
INTELLIGENCE SUMMARY.

(Erase heading not required.)

Instructions regarding War Diaries and Intelligence Summaries are contained in F. S. Regs., Part II. and the Staff Manual respectively. Title pages will be prepared in manuscript.

Place	Date 1918 Novr	Hour	Summary of Events and Information	Remarks and references to Appendices
AVESNES	25th		Battalion paraded at 10.5 hours and proceeded by route march to billets in CAMBRAI.	
CAMBRAI	26th		Resting and generally cleaning up	
"	27th 28th		Training under Company arrangements.	
"	29th		Battalion paraded at 0830 hours and proceeded by lorry from CAMBRAI to billets in FIEFES & MONTRELET in the CANDAS Area arriving at about 1830 hours.	
FIEFES	30th		Day spent in generally cleaning up of billets etc.	

C. L. Bean
Lieut. Colonel
Commanding 2nd Bn Wiltshire Regiment.

CONFIDENTIAL

WAR DIARY

of

2nd BN WILTSHIRE REGIMENT

FROM 1st to 31st DECEMBER 1918.

VOLUME 51.

WAR DIARY
or
INTELLIGENCE SUMMARY.
(Erase heading not required.)

Army Form C. 2118.

Instructions regarding War Diaries and Intelligence Summaries are contained in F. S. Regs., Part II. and the Staff Manual respectively. Title pages will be prepared in manuscript.

Place	Date	Hour	Summary of Events and Information	Remarks and references to Appendices
	1918			
FIFFFS.	Dec 1		Sunday - Church Parade.	
	" 2		Training under Company arrangements. Football in afternoon.	
	" 3			
	" 4		"A" & "C" Coys - Route March. "B" & "D" Coys Platoon and Company Drill - All available N.C.O's drilled under R.S.M.	
	W 5		"B" & "D" Coys route March - "A" & "C" Coys Company Drill.	
	" 6		Training under Company arrangements. Educational Classes and Lewis Gun Instruction.	
	" 7			
	" 8		Section and Platoon Drill - Musketry instruction. Educational Classes.	
	" 9		2 Companies route march - 2 Coys training under their own arrangements. "C" Coy played "D" Coy in Brigade Inter Coy Competition the latter winning by 2 goals to 1.	
	" 10.		"A" & "B" Coys route march. "C" & "D" Coys Lewis gun and Musketry Instruction.	
	" 11		Training under Company arrangements.	
	" 12.		Battalion moved by route march to billets at St LEGER.	
St Leger.	" 13		Training as usual. Capt F.H. BONE M.C. Joined Battalion for duty and took over Command of "A" Coy. Lt Col P.S.L. BEAVER M.C. proceeded to England to attend course of Instruction at CAMBERLEY - Major W.S. SHEPHERD M.C. assuming Command of the Battalion.	
	" 14		Kit inspections - Platoon Drill and Musketry Instruction. Education Classes continued.	
	" 15		Sunday - Church Parade.	
	" 16.		"A" & "B" Coys route march - "C" & "D" Coys musketry instruction on range. Educational Classes as usual.	
	" 17.		Training under Company arrangements - Educational Classes and Lewis Gun Instruction.	

Army Form C. 2118.

WAR DIARY
or
INTELLIGENCE SUMMARY.
(Erase heading not required.)

Instructions regarding War Diaries and Intelligence Summaries are contained in F. S. Regs., Part II. and the Staff Manual respectively. Title pages will be prepared in manuscript.

Place	Date 1918	Hour	Summary of Events and Information	Remarks and references to Appendices
ST LEGER.	Decr 18.		"C" & "D" Coys route march - "A" & "B" Coys musketry instruction on range. Education Classes.	
	19) 20) 21)		Training under Company arrangements. Education Classes. Football etc in afternoons.	
	22.		Sunday - Church Parade.	
	23.		Musketry Instruction on range for "D" & "C" Coys. "A" & "B" Coys carrying out Box respirator Drill - Lewis Gun Instruction and Physical Training.	
	24.		Musketry Instruction and Lewis Gun Classes.	
	25		XMAS DAY - Battalion Concert Party gave a performance to the whole Battalion in the Theatre at St LEGER in the evening.	
	26.		Route march under Company arrangements.	
	27) 28)		Training under Company arrangements. Annual Dinner for Sergeants held on night of 28th.	
	29.		Sunday - Church Parade.	
	30.		"A" "C" & "D" Coys route march - "B" Coy carried out musketry instruction.	
	31		Training under Company arrangements. Regimental Dinner was held in the Girls School St LEGER - Guests were, Lt Col R.M.T. GILLSON D.S.O, Lt Col L.F. SMEATHMAN D.S.O., Lt Col H.L. JONES D.S.O.	

Major
Commanding 2nd Bn Wiltshire Regiment.

Confidential

War Diary

of

2nd Bn Wiltshire Regiment

From 1st to 31st January 1919

Volume 52.

WAR DIARY
INTELLIGENCE SUMMARY.
(Erase heading not required.)

Army Form C. 2118.

Instructions regarding War Diaries and Intelligence Summaries are contained in F. S. Regs., Part II. and the Staff Manual respectively. Title pages will be prepared in manuscript.

Place	Date 1919	Hour	Summary of Events and Information	Remarks and references to Appendices
ST LEGER	1st Jany	-	Musketry & Lewis Gun Instruction - Baths	
"	2nd "	"	'E' Coys attend 50 yards range - A.D.B Coys gave Musketry & Lewis Gun Instruction and Physical Training	
"	3rd "		Training under Company arrangements	
"	4th "		Battalion Parade for "TROOPING of the COLOURS"	
"	5th "		Sunday - Church Parade	
"	6th "		B Company Musketry Instruction. Firing on 50 yards range - B. C. & D Coys Company Drill and Physical Training.	
"	7th "		B Company firing on range - A.C.&D Coys Company Drill & Physical Training.	
"	8th "		C Company on range. A.B.&D Coys Musketry Lewis Gun Instruction	
"	9th "		D Company on range - A.B.&C Coys Company Drill & Physical Training	
"	10th "		All Companies Route march	
"	11th "		Kit Inspection - Six separate Drill & Company Drill & Company Drill. Major A. Carthwaite & 20 N.C. joined on duty.	
"	12th "		Sunday - Church Parade.	
"	13th "		Squads under Company arrangements. Baths	
"	14th "		E Coy attend 50 yards range - A.B. & C Coys Musketry Lewis Gun Instruction & Physical Training. 2/Lt E.C. Hunton proceeded to Nth Corps Concentration Camp for Demobilization.	

JANUARY 1919 . Sheet No 1.

Army Form C. 2118.

WAR DIARY
or
INTELLIGENCE SUMMARY.
(Erase heading not required.)

Instructions regarding War Diaries and Intelligence Summaries are contained in F. S. Regs., Part II. and the Staff Manual respectively. Title pages will be prepared in manuscript.

Place	Date	Hour	Summary of Events and Information	Remarks and references to Appendices
	1919 JAN'Y			
ST LEGER	15"		Inter Coton Company arrangements. A Coy allotted 50 yds range. Musketry course 2/Lt C Lager MC Proceeded to Corps Concentration Camp for demobilisation. Same course.	
"	16"		B Coy allotted 50 yds range and Assault Course.	
"	17"		Company Competition for Drill Turn out & Musketry.	
"	18"		B Coy firing on range. Company Competition - Bullet + Bayonet Competition to	
"	19"		Company Games - Lancs - Church Parade	
"	20"		Company Competition continued. B + C Coys firing on range - Service Parade for Presentation of Colours to 9 RWF by Lieut on Guards Parade Ground. "H" Company 2/Lts being detailed to keep the ground - Major R Latham BSO MC proceeded to 25" Bn HQ on appointment as Brigade Education Officer.	
"	21"		B Company firing on Company Competition - Both allotted to A.B.+C. Companies	
"	22/"		Both for 2. Coy HQ Coy + transport - Parade for Presentation of Colours to 9 RWF and O Guard Regt held on Guards Parade Ground - A Coy 2nd/Lts being detailed to keep the Ground - B.C.+D Coys attended as spectators. Remr of Company	
"			Rugger Coy Ground - A Coy finals. B Coy Sports. D Coy sports. C Coy finals. A.B+C. Coys Musketry Course Lewis Gun Instructor -	
"	28"		D Company allotted 50 yards range - A.B+C Coys Musketry Course Lewis Gun Instructor - Battalion Played 3rd Worcester Regt at FIENVILLERS in Divisional Football Competition - Worcesters winning 2 goals to nil.	

JANUARY 1919 - Sheet no 2.

WAR DIARY
or
INTELLIGENCE SUMMARY.

(Erase heading not required.)

Army Form C. 2118.

Place	Date	Hour	Summary of Events and Information	Remarks and references to Appendices
St LEGER	1919 May 24		Route March under Company arrangements	
"	25		His Subsection - Box Respirator Drill & Company drill	
"	26		Church Parade - Lieutenant Col Davis rar-Roux proceeded to XVII Corps Concentration Camp for Demobilisation	
"	27		Route March under Coy arrangements	
"	28		Lecture to Battalion in Concert Hall St LEGER on "Famous British Cavalry Leaders" Drill & Bayonet Training	
"	29		All Companies: Musketry, Lewis Gun Instruction & Bayonet Training	
"	30		Musketry, Lewis Gun Instruction & Bayonet training. His Subsection Box Respirator & Company Drill	
"	31		During the month slow and morning was devoted to General Classes. Football Recreation in the afternoon. The Battalion concert party "THE NINES" gave performances periodically to the Battalion and other units of the 58: Brigade.	

P. L. Beaver Lt Col.
Comdg 2nd Yorkshire Regiment

Confidential

War diary

of

2.B⁰ Wiltshire Regiment

From 1st to 28 February 1919.

Volume. 52.

WAR DIARY
or
INTELLIGENCE SUMMARY.
(Erase heading not required.)

Army Form C. 2118.

Place	Date 1919	Hour	Summary of Events and Information	Remarks and references to Appendices
ST. LEGER.	Feb 1st		Kit Inspection - Box Respirator Drill & Saluting Drill.	
"	" 2nd		Sunday - Church Parade	
"	" 3rd		Grades under Company arrangements. Baths - Lecture by Brigade Education Officer which all Company Commanders and Battalion Education Instructor attended.	
"	" 4th		Physical Training & Saluting Drill. Baths.	
"	" 5th		Battalion Route March.	
"	" 6th		All available men employed in clearing the snow from the principal streets in the village.	
"	" 7th		Battalion Parade - Physical Training & Saluting Drill.	
"	" 8th		Kit Inspection - Box Respirator Drill - Physical Training.	
"	" 9th		Sunday. Church Parade.	
"	" 10th		All available men employed in clearing the main road of the village - 48.4 the Prince of Wales passed through the village.	
"	" 11th		Practice Guards Parade - Physical Training for all other available men. The Battalion Brass Band joined the Battalion from England.	
"	" 12th & 13th		Battalion Route March.	

WAR DIARY
or
INTELLIGENCE SUMMARY.
(Erase heading not required.)

Army Form C. 2118.

Instructions regarding War Diaries and Intelligence Summaries are contained in F. S. Regs., Part II. and the Staff Manual respectively. Title pages will be prepared in manuscript.

Place	Date 1919	Hour	Summary of Events and Information	Remarks and references to Appendices
ST. LEGER	Feb 14		Battalion Route March – Capt A.W. Lacoste proceeded to England for 2 months Leave –	
"	" 15		Kit inspection – Box respirator drill – Lt B? Reninow M.M. proceeded to England for 2 months Leave.	
"	" 16		Sunday – Church Parade. Capt A.B.M. Welford M.C. proceeded to England on 2 months Leave.	
"	" 17		Grand Practise Parade – Lecture by Col Raynor DSO on the "British Dominions" to the Battalion – Capt S.V. Aulton M.C. B.M. proceeded to England on 2 months Leave.	
"	" 18		Battalion Route March – Capt P.P. Legg M.C. proceeded to England on 2 months Leave.	
"	" 19		Battalion Route March.	
"	" 20		All available men employed on cleaning up the billeting area.	
"	" 21			
"	" 22			
"	" 23		Sunday – Church Parade.	
"	" 24		Battalion paraded at 10.15 and proceeded in Lorries to new camp at VILLERS L'HOPITAL.	

WAR DIARY
or
INTELLIGENCE SUMMARY.

Army Form C. 2118.

Place	Date	Hour	Summary of Events and Information	Remarks and references to Appendices
VILLERS L'HOPITAL	Feb 25/26		All available men employed in cleaning up camp.	
"	27.		Lieutenants C.A. Pocock and J.A.T.D. CAREY together with a draft of 12th other ranks proceeded by train from CANDAS to ROUEN for transfer to 1/5 Gloucester Regt. to form part of the Army of Occupation in Germany.	
"	28.		By this date, owing to continued Demobilisation during the months and the departure of the draft the 27th, the Battalion was reduced to almost Cadre strength. Strength on this date was 19 Officers and 111 other ranks, which included the Battalion band of 36 other ranks.	

P.L. Bearn
Lieut Col
Comdg 2/8th Worceste Regt.